# Fashion

## COLORING BOOK

## For Girls

This BOOK
Belongs to:

Ajl liy

- - - - - - - - - - - - - - - - - - - -

- - - - - - - - - - - - - - - - - - - -

I'm
OK!

casual fashion

Best
FRIENDS
ever

edu
F h n

California
LO
VE
Best
FRIENDS
ever

Paris
France

Rock

Music is
what
feelings
sound
like.

# Cool Girl

Fashion

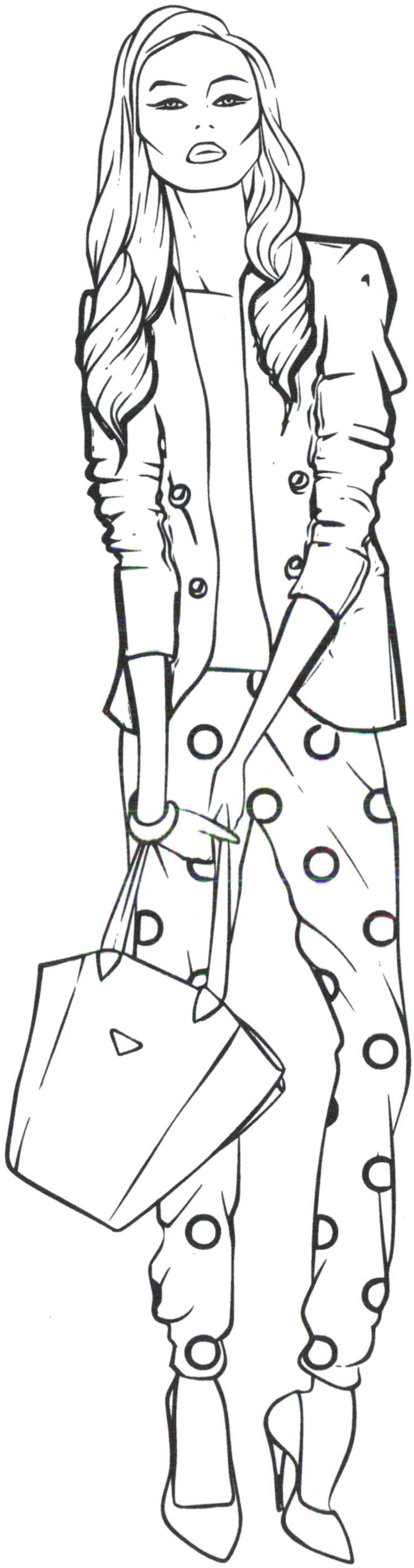

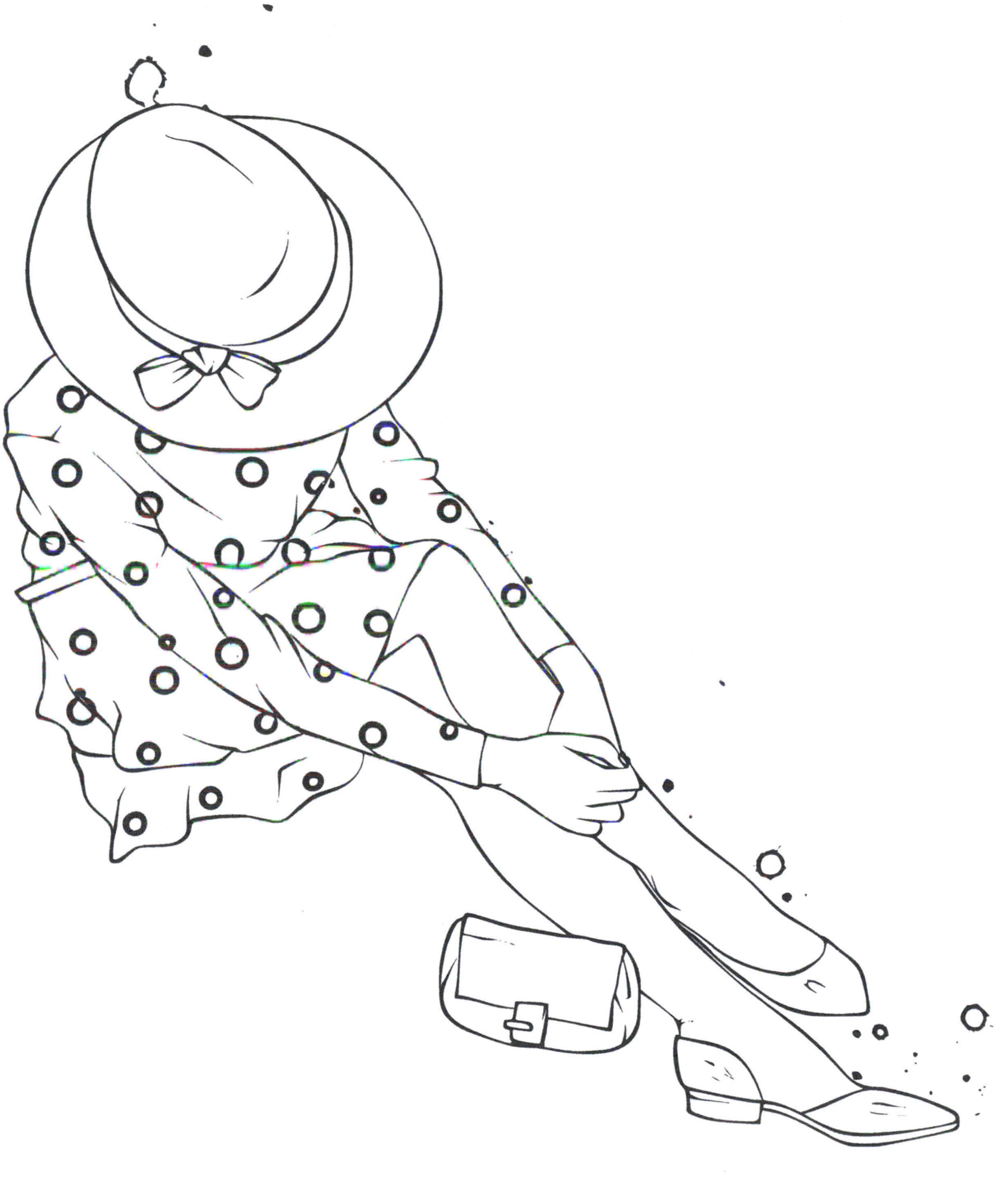

Paris
France

# Winter Bruges

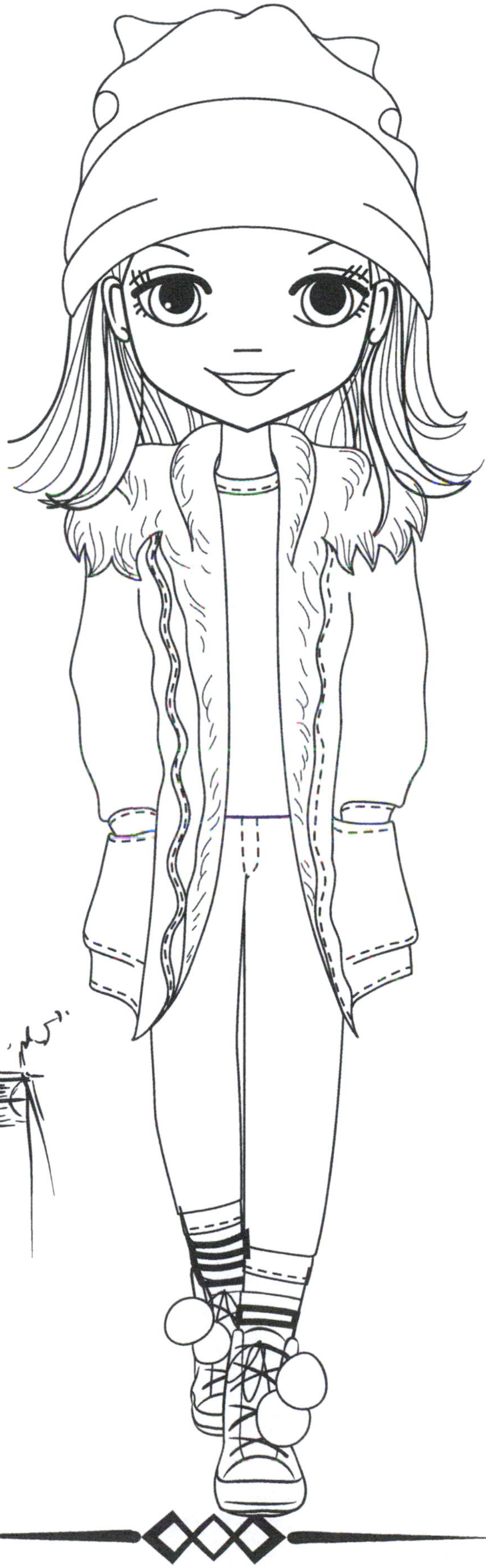

LOVELY

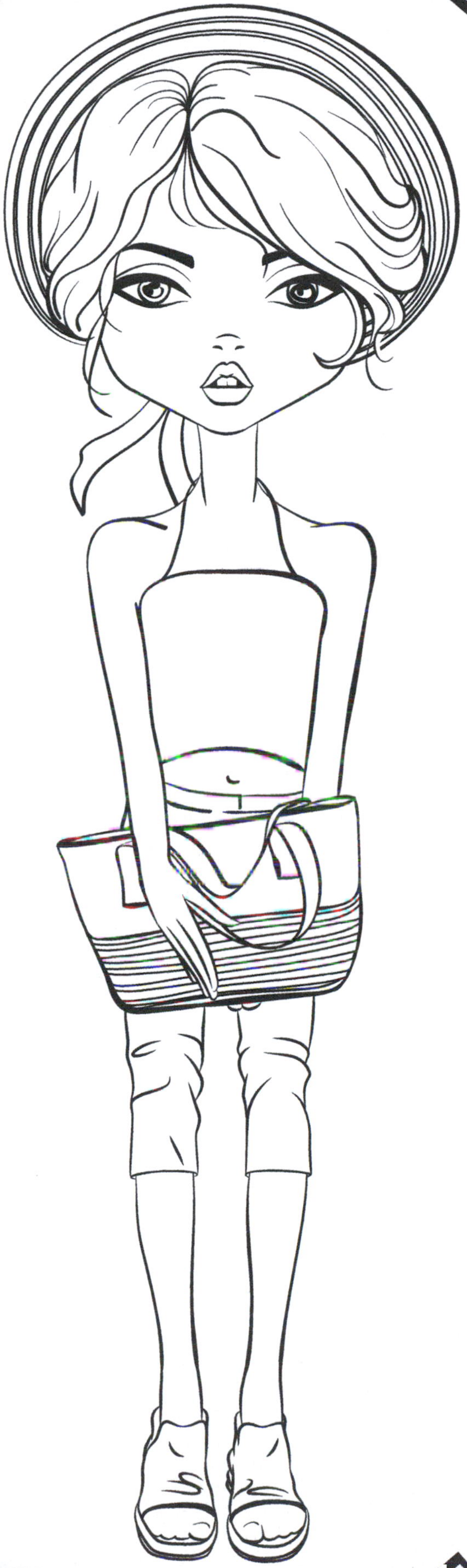

I love traveling light...
N
W
E
S